Rewire Your Habits

Establish Goals, Evolve Your Habits, And Improve
Your Relationships, Health, Finances,
And Free Time

By Zoe McKey

Communication Coach and Social Development
Trainer

zoemckey@gmail.com
www.zoemckey.com

Thank you for choosing my book! I would like to show my appreciation for the trust you gave me by giving **FREE GIFTS** for you!

For more information visit www.zoemckey.com

The checklist talks about *5 key elements of building self-confidence* and contains extra actionable worksheets with practice exercises for deeper learning.

Learn how to:

- Solve 80% of you self-esteem issues with one simple change
- Keep your confidence permanent without falling back to self-doubt
- Not fall into the trap of promising words
- Overcome anxiety
- Be confident among other people

The cheat sheet teaches you three key daily routine techniques to become more productive, have less stress in your life, and be more well-balanced. It also has a step-by-step sample sheet that you can fill in with your daily routines.

Discover how to:

- Overcome procrastination following 8 simple steps
- Become more organized
- Design your yearly, monthly, weekly and daily tasks in the most productive way.
- 3 easy tricks to level up your mornings

author shall not be liable for damages arising herefrom. The fact that an individual, organization of website is referred to in this work as a citation and/or potential source of further information does not mean that the author endorses the information the individual, organization to website may provide or recommendations they/it may make. Further, readers should be aware that Internet websites listed in this work might have changed or disappeared between when this work was written and when it is read.

For general information on the products and services or to obtain technical support, please contact the author.

Table Of Contents

Introduction

It's Monday, the first day of a new month, your birthday, and Mars closes an optimal orbit with Mercury, so you've decided this is the perfect time to get the perfect body.

You've procrastinated on this matter for a long time, coming up with excuses like the fact that it's holiday season, you have a hectic job schedule, or your dog is sick to delay the moment of starting a diet. But now you've seen or heard something groundbreaking, and besides, it's Monday, the first day of the month...

So the time has come to become that flawless, lean, Lulu-pants-wearing or muscle-tank-wearing person you always dreamed of being. You're excited. In a little while the street will become your catwalk, heads will turn after your graceful or bulky march, and Karl Lagerfeld will reach out to you on social media to beg you to promote his humble creations. *Okay, time to get back to earth. This all sounds cool, but how do you want to achieve all these grandiose goals?*

If you're like most people, you already have your diet carefully planned in your head from today to the day you're supposed to reach your goal. You've selected a diet plan, the strictest of them all, and are starting it right away because you *"ain't like other losers who give it up after two weeks of painful fasting."* You were born a fighter, so you'll fight. The *Mission: Impossible* soundtrack is echoing in your head as you start your badass diet. Day one, tick. Day two, tick. Whoa, two pounds gone! Mostly water, but who cares? Day nine, seven pounds gone. If you continue at this speed, you'll reach your target weight quicker than expected!

Day twenty, nine pounds gone. Life feels miserable, weight loss slows down, and you miss your dandy candies and soda at the end of each hard day. You're hungry and irritable. If only you could have a piece of chocolate. Just one. Just a little…

No! You remind yourself of your goal, your

strength, and turning heads on the street. The *Mission: Impossible* theme is silent in your head. Queen meekly hums *The Show Must Go On* instead.

Some long months have passed and you've made it halfway through your weight loss endeavors. You feel like you've been drained of life essence. You look somewhat better now. Not catwalk good, but thirty pounds less than before. If you invest more time and at least the same effort, within a year you could — maybe, possibly but not surely — get your dream body. You go to work, trying to make peace with this thought. Later that day, your boss fires you and you feel that life sucks in a superlative sense, and as you hysterically run out of your office, you spot a new KFC at the corner. *Don't Stop Me Now* powerfully resounds in your head as you approach the wicked fast food chain.

Your proverbial angels try to stop you, but you eat them as appetizers. Without being very conscious about your actions, you order two large meals, a *diet Coke*, and since it doesn't really make a difference, a cookie too.

There were weeks when you didn't eat as many calories as with this one meal. Your stomach happily growls as it expands to accept all the long-desired sins you just shoveled down your throat. As the meal disappears, so do your dreams about having that beach body. You find comfort in the thirty pounds lost, but since you stop caring, the nasty weight sneaks back to your body before you know it.

There are not too many success stories in excessive weight loss. Maybe for a good reason. Most people approach diet as the necessary evil that helps them lose pounds within a certain timeframe. The sooner, the better. They starve themselves, become unpredictable and fickle, and any type of tragedy can deter them from their goal.

The other type of people, those few who actually reach their target, have a different mindset. They know that absolute denial of daily pleasures will drive them crazy at some point. They also know that they need a lifelong lifestyle change instead of a short-term diet to preserve their good results.

Many goals we set in our lives are just like trying to lose weight. We want our reward quickly, and in the moment of setting the goal, we don't really care how difficult it will be on day seventy-three. YOLO! Then we find ourselves choking on a Big Mac on day forty-nine. Or we find ourselves not willing to work out for a year. Or that nothing remained in our active-passive memory from that boring management course.

Why? Because we approached improvement the wrong way. We often do. There is, however, an alternative way to approach your goals. This book will tell you about it in detail.

Chapter 1: The Real Purpose Of Goal Setting

"If I were rich, I'd buy this car, travel to that island, buy nicer clothes…"

Do you hear this often? Do you say it often? And when you ask yourself or the person you're talking to, "Why not now?" does the answer sound something like this:

"I can't afford it now." Or, "My current job doesn't pay me enough." Or, "The circumstances are not ideal right now for me to make a change."

The time isn't right to become wealthier? To do something you really like? When is the ideal time then? I saw a picture of a circle divided into three parts — health, time, and money. Then the advice next to it is: pick two.

Why? Why couldn't you have them all? Indeed, with a pick two mentality, you'll never have all the three. Now, you may think, *I am already sixty-five. I am old.* You are as old as you believe yourself to be. A young reader might think, *I'm only seventeen. How can I become successful so early?*

You can't have it all. But you can have more health, wealth, and time than you do now. But how badly do you want it? Why do people fail to reach their goals?

Sometimes the cause is simply that people don't take themselves seriously. With words, they'd be able to conquer an empire, but when it comes to their actions, they can't even reach the remote control on the coffee table. They long for a better life, but they won't get off the couch for it. If words are not followed by actions, they are merely fantasies.

Waiting for the right moment is another sure route to an unfulfilled life. Many people don't want to take responsibility for their actions, and they expect their dream life to just happen at some point. The greatest action they take is to come up with excuses as to why they can't or won't make the changes today. The smarter the person, the better the excuse. But again, no change will follow excuses.

"What's the point of doing it, of deceiving myself? I won't be able to realize it, anyway." People lack self-confidence and don't know how or where to start the change. They fear rejection and other people's judgment.

Another fear that hinders people from setting goals is the fear of failure. But without failure, there is no success, just like without darkness, there is no light. The more things you start, the greater your chances for succeeding.

I had a conversation with a friend recently. He was very fat a few years ago. Now he works out regularly and has lost a lot of weight. His goal was to look like Hugh Jackman. I don't need to mention how his gym mates reacted when he became vocal about his goal. Two years ago it sounded funny to me too, to be honest. Now that his body actually resembles the Australian actor's, I find his efforts admirable, especially because he persisted when nobody believed in him. He paid the price of his goal — total lifestyle change, strict diet, daily workout — and now everybody respects him for it. I asked him how he could be so sure he'd reach his goal. "Weren't you afraid of failure?" I asked.

"You never fail," he said. "You succeed, or you learn."

By setting and pursuing goals, you have nothing to lose but a lot to gain. It has been scientifically proven that people who set goals are more fulfilled and positive about life. Having a purpose to wake up to each day will challenge us and give us meaning.

There are, however, some more skeptical views on goal setting. In the book *Goals Gone Wild: The Systematic Side Effects of Overprescribing Goal Setting* by Ordóñez, L. D., Schweitzer, M. E., Galinsky, A. D., & Bazerman, M. H., the authors argue that people rely too much on the hope that their self-discipline and willpower will outlast their lost motivation toward their goals. We are human; we make calculation errors, especially when it comes to goals. In the heat of the moment, we tend to set bigger goals than we could realistically achieve. We don't have the necessary skills, knowledge, or devotion to see them through. And when we don't make the expected progress with them, we become frustrated.

Sometimes we turn to easy solutions, or "life hacks." But these shortcuts won't get us anywhere closer to our goal on the long run. Why? Because we may lose those pounds fast with the sunshine diet, but as soon as we start eating like an actual human, those nasty pounds will crawl back. We may cheat on our math test, but that won't save us on the SATs.

The authors of the book suggest focusing on setting one's mind on habit creation instead of goal setting.

We don't like to set small goals. Why small, right? You'll accomplish it before you know it. We like to set grandiose, challenging goals instead like losing thirty pounds in half a year, or doubling your income in a month. The thing is, these goals hardly ever stick because they require a lot of focus, effort, and willpower. They require so much that chances are you'll run out of steam before you get to that proverbial finish line. You'll find yourself right where you started with the whole goal setting process, plus you'll be carrying a sense of failure as bonus.

It is much more rewarding to invest our limited time and willpower in building useful habits that can help us achieve our goals without requiring too much effort. Think of it this way: When you were a toddler and you could hardly walk, it was your goal to get to the corner shop on your own. When you learned walking, you could go to the corner shop without even thinking about it. You were not cheering yourself on anymore with mantras of, "Let's go to the corner shop. Left foot, right foot, left foot…" You were just there. This is how I could illustrate the simplest way the difference between goals and habits.

Goals, however, beat habits in one area: they sound much cooler. They're much more motivating in the moment we set them. Imagining how your goal will slowly unfold and become reality is intriguing. Doing this, doing that, learning this, learning that… The process of acquiring habits, on the other hand, is rather dull. Who likes to daydream about repeating the same action each day at ten a.m., right? That's why we set goals instead.

But goals don't grant you continuity. That's why so many people gain the weight back after finishing their diet. They don't have a sturdy new lifestyle. They just focused on their goal, then they reached it. Now what? Let's eat! They have no well-formed habit to keep up the healthy lifestyle that affords them their beach body.

Habits are never-ending goals, if you think about it. They have no deadline and no end point. They are casual daily activities like brushing your teeth or combing your hair. The brain gets tired of goals — each day, it becomes more burdensome to keep up the "spirit." Habits are not difficult to form. For example, if you don't brush your teeth you'll feel awkward all day, swallowing economy-sized Tic Tac boxes just to make up for your missed routine.

This being said, you can still have goals. You can still aim to double your income. Put your goal on a paper. Then shift your focus from strictly pursuing the goal to developing habits that enforce your goal. Create habits that make your goal inevitable. Do you want to double your income? Make it a habit to research alternative money-making methods, or methods that teach you how to work smarter. Pledge to engage in productivity habits. While you practice them, your income will gradually grow as a side-effect.

The life-changing magic of habit stacking

Charles Duhigg in his book *The Power of Habit* and Steve Scott in *Habit Stacking* explored the phenomenon that some habits are better than others, or are more useful to acquire, for the simple reason they attract other optimal habits into your life.

For example, jogging or running is not only great cardio, but research proves that it also helps you quitting smoking. If you habitually jog each day, your willingness to smoke will decrease, maybe because otherwise your lungs would give up.

These habits, called as "keystone habits," will make it easier to adopt other good habits with less effort, once acquired. What can be a good "keystone habit"?

Let's take health goals as an example. We all would like to be healthier, thinner, age slower, be more mentally active, and so on. What habit could aid you with all these goals?

Fitness specialists, doctors, researchers all agree on the beneficial effect of weight-lifting. Not the crazy, screaming, three-hundred-pound weight-lifting — just the regular out-of-the-comfort-zone kind. Investing time and effort in weight-lifting is very rewarding. You will get stronger. Your endurance and mental toughness will grow, too. You'll be fitter and more energetic.

A study at Harvard University showed that the effort you make while lifting weights triggers the release of beneficial hormones like endorphins, adrenaline, and serotonin. Weight-lifting, due to the heavy physical effort you make, will slow down cell atrophy, and therefore reduce the effects of aging. It also raises your metabolism and helps you digest food better. Your brain will be more aware and you'll focus better.

As you can see, just by adopting this one activity as a habit, many areas of your life will benefit.

If you're wondering how you can start building habits, the answer is simple: Start small. Take one small action at the time. I call it a **SMACKTION** (small smacking action) to kick yourself out of your comfort zone and start doing what needs to be done. Make sure to follow the SMACKTION with a **SNACKTION** (small snack in action).

For example: After you're finished with your first weight-lifting session, reward yourself with a yummy protein shake. It is healthy(ish) and helps your muscles' recovery.

Some research argues that a habit can stick in thirty days, while other researchers say that adopting a new habit can take as long as two hundred and fifty-four days. Whoever is right, it is not my business to decide. I invite you to set thirty-day challenges to adopt a habit.

What does this mean? It means that you have to pick a useful habit you'd like to adopt into your daily life. This habit can be health-, wealth-, relationship-, or free time-related. Do your best effort for thirty days to install the habit of your choice into your daily life. If you feel that the habit didn't stick in thirty days (if it sticks it becomes an automatic activity, you don't really have to concentrate doing it), set another thirty-day challenge and keep up the good work on adopting the habit of your choice. Repeat the monthly challenges until you succeed.

Look at the monthly challenges as you look at Parkinson's Law: "Work expands so as to fill the time available for its completion." If you give yourself too long to accomplish something, you won't even start working on it until half the time has passed. This is the main issue with New Year's resolutions, by the way — you give yourself a year to change your life. Chances are you won't start acting on it until July or so. Then you run out of time.

Monthly challenges give you a sense of urgency. A month is long enough to accomplish something, but short enough that you can't just sit on your butt.

I hope by now you see what the real purpose of goal setting is. It serves to give you direction on what habits should you incorporate into your life. These habits will lead you to reach your goal with less effort. After you know where you want to go, don't focus on the goal.

Saying "I want to be twenty-five pounds skinnier in four months" or "I want to get a boyfriend before Christmas" and then forcing yourself into a myriad of actions you hate doing, working out sixty hours a week or going on two Tinder dates daily, will make you feel miserable. Even if you reach your goal, it won't make you happy, and like someone who won easy money, you'll sabotage yourself.

Forget linear progress — aim for exponential progress instead. Make small steps toward your better future. When you reach a milestone in your plans, invest this growth into another rewarding prospect. Like weight-lifting. Remember? Incorporate weight-lifting into your daily workout. When weight-lifting works well, take it to the next level — make it a habit to eat food that will help you make the most of your weight-lifting efforts.

Choose to start adopting the habit which has the highest rate of return first. This way you'll jumpstart the improvement in more life areas.

You can stack the other, smaller habits to get to the big one later. For example, starting with eating food that helps weight-lifting without lifting weights is a bit purposeless and demotivating. You get the gist.

After a lot of research and thinking, I chose to elaborate on five major life areas where you could and should incorporate good habits. These life areas are: personal development, relationships, health, finances and free time.

Chapter 2: Energy Management

Everyone is short on time. But there is something that is even more limited than our time: our energy. Let's be optimistic and have plans for the next forty, fifty, even sixty years. Time is running out, but the energy we have every day is much more limited.

There are countless self-help books and articles out there which try to offer you tips and techniques for successful time management. However, they may be leading you down a less productive path. Research now suggests that it is more important for us to focus on managing our energy rather than struggling to manage time, which often proves elusive and, since it comes in a finite amount, is nearly impossible to truly manage. In our fast-paced, busy lives, it is natural to think that if we push ourselves harder we should be able to accomplish more, but it is impossible to be productive if we try to keep high energy levels all throughout our entire day.

A day consists of twenty-four hours, but we simply can't function at energy level ten 100% of the time. Not long-term, at least. We need to work smarter, not harder. We start our day with a certain energy level each morning. It rises to a point; studies say that this point is around eleven a.m. for a person who sleeps eight hours and wakes around seven a.m. Depending on your sleeping schedule, your high-energy zone may be different. For somebody who wakes between seven and eight a.m., the high-energy zone will last until eleven a.m. After that, it will decrease. I call this the 7/11 rule: wake up at seven, seven days a week, and finish your most important tasks before eleven a.m.

Nutrition plays a very important role in how much energy you have during the day. The average person is careless in the morning. They don't eat breakfast, or only eat a minimal amount of food. Then around noon, they eat a gigantic lunch and knock themselves out, energetically, for at least two hours. Why? Because they start digesting like an anaconda after eating a crocodile. The brain will be busy digesting the crocodile.

Schedule your work to coordinate with your energy levels.

Take a week to monitor your energy fluctuation. This means you need to pay attention on an hourly basis to how energized you feel. Ten is very energized, one is on the verge of sleep. Log your energy level in a journal every hour beginning the hour you wake up and ending the hour you go to sleep. It's a bit fussy, but the reward is worth your time.

It's important to keep your regular daily routine. Don't try to alter your results. Just do everything as you usually do — plus monitor your energy level. The goal is to find which periods of the day you feel most energized during following your normal routines. You'll be surprised by the discoveries you make. If you follow the same eating and sleeping routine each day, you'll see that your most energetic periods fall in the same time frame every day.

After you've identified your high, medium, and low energy level zones, arrange your daily tasks so the most important are done in the first high energy period, and the low priority tasks in the low energy periods.

Schedule your work around your energy level.
When you decide to change your life, you want to change everything immediately, right? You want to change your behavior, habits, health routines, your relationships — everything. But you will end up changing nothing because you won't be able to follow all these sudden changes.

Maxwell Maltz, a plastic surgeon, concluded that patients need twenty-one days to recover and get familiar with the changes after a plastic surgery. He popularized the concept that breaking a habit and replacing it with another takes twenty-one days. However, a study from University College London proved that the number of days might vary between eighteen and two hundred fifty-four, depending on the individual. Something becomes a habit when you don't have to focus on doing it anymore. In our case, when you can go through a day without putting extra effort into positioning your tasks to conform to your energy level, you can move to the "schedule your work around your energy level" phase.

This means that you have to be conscious of your sleeping and eating habits. A complete lifestyle change is necessary. Here are some of the most important aspects:

Sleep at least seven hours.

"Eat breakfast like a king, lunch like a prince, and dinner like a pauper." This is from the famous nutritionist Adele Davis. I highly recommend her books as a guide for lifestyle changes.

Avoid the "white poisons," namely sugar, flour, salt, and milk.

When it comes to carbs, the more complex, the better. Stick to vegetables or whole grains that contain lots of fiber. Refined carbohydrates, like sugary products, are not your friends.

Help your digestive system by combining foods in a way that makes them easier for your stomach to digest. Avoid eating proteins with starches.

Proteins require an acidic medium for digestion. This acid neutralizes the alkaline medium necessary for starch digestion. Thus, you will end up with indigestion from fermentation. You'll feel heavy and exhausted.

Here is some more good advice from the top nutritionists in the world: Starches, green vegetables, sugars, and fat can be eaten together. They need either an alkaline or neutral medium for digestion. Proteins, acidic fruits (like citrus), and green vegetables can also be eaten together as they require an acid or neutral medium for their digestion. Starches and proteins, as well as acid fruits and fats, shouldn't be combined in a meal if you want the best results from the food you've eaten. For more information about food combining, read the works of Jeremy E. Kaslow, MD, FACP, FACAAI physician and surgeon.

Exercise for at least twenty minutes each day.

Energy management needs a lot of attention and persistence; nevertheless, it's worth it. You will not only have a healthier lifestyle, but your energy level will be more stable. Of all the body's internal functions, digestion requires the most energy.

Now think about your own life. When do you feel that you are under the most stress? If you are like the average person, it is probably when you feel like you are running out of time and can't stay on schedule to finish what you started.

When we allow ourselves to get stressed out because we feel like our time is running out, our ability to think clearly decreases greatly. By managing our energy wisely, we can change our stress levels and productivity. If we focus on the things we can control, we will start to see an improvement in all aspects of our daily lives.

Scientific research backs up the importance of energy management as well. The Federal Aviation Administration conducted a study which found that taking short breaks during long work sessions caused a 16% improvement in employees' focus and awareness.

Why is this? Taking breaks is actually following your body's natural rhythm. Nathaniel Kleitman, a physiologist and the sleep researcher who codiscovered REM sleep, is famous for finding that we alternate between light and deep sleep in ninety-minute increments. Kleitman also went on to find that our bodies follow the same ninety-minute rhythm during the day as we move between periods of being more and less alert.

According to Tony Schwartz, in his article in the Harvard Business Review, after people work very intensely for longer than ninety minutes, they begin to rely on stress hormones as their source of energy. He writes that the prefrontal cortex of the brain starts to shut down and people begin to struggle to think clearly.

Too often, people try to counteract these natural periods of low energy by consuming caffeine or sugary foods. Any energy boost one receives from consuming these foods or drinks is short-lived, so people may be better served by following their bodies' natural rhythm and taking short breaks to rest and regroup.

Research on ultradian rhythms conducted by Peretz Lavie agrees with these findings. When people work productively for ninety minutes and then take a short fifteen- to twenty-minute break, they are acting more in sync with their bodies' natural energy cycles and are able to stay focused and maintain higher energy levels throughout the day.

This cycle is being followed by people in all different professional fields. Some of the most talented violinists in the world share the common schedule of practicing their instrument intensely for ninety minutes and then taking a fifteen-minute break.

The U.S. Army Research Institute also conducted a study which found that people have better focus and increased levels of energy for longer amounts of time when they work for ninety minutes and then take a twenty-minute break.

Dr. Alejandro Lleras, a psychology professor at the University of Illinois, believes it is crucial for people to schedule occasional breaks from their work, regardless of how they decide to spend their few minutes of rest. A study was conducted on eighty-four subjects who were expected to perform a simple task on the computer for an hour. The people who were allowed to take two short breaks during that time had a consistent performance through the whole hour, while the people who weren't given a break saw a decrease in their performance over time. After our bodies and minds are exposed to stimulation for an extended period of time, our brains begin to view the stimulus as being unimportant and our minds erase it from our awareness. Taking a break is imperative in order for our brains to view the stimulus as being new enough to allow us to focus on it again.

A big part of being conscious of your energy levels means living in the present moment and being connected to your body. The better you are able to know your mind and your body and how they are linked, the more productive you will be in your daily life. Most people have times of the day when they feel more mentally sharp and focused and have more physical energy. If you learn to plan your schedule around those peak performance periods, you may find that your day can be much more productive.

While not everyone's body has the exact same circadian rhythms of high and low functionality, there are often similar times of day for many people. As previously discussed, it is common for many to find it hardest to concentrate and stay focused between the hours of twelve to four p.m. Studies have found that the brain is typically best at dealing with difficult cognitive tasks once the body has been fed and the brain has had a chance to become fully awake. Focus your intense energy levels on the most difficult tasks in the late morning and then factor in a break in the afternoon during the times of most distraction (lunch).

Creative thinking has been shown to increase during the afternoon hours for many people, so allowing yourself some time to think about problems which may require some creativity to solve during that time period may prove to be productive.

While it would be nice if we could all wave a magic wand and make the stress in our lives disappear, unfortunately, it is simply not possible to erase all our stress. However, we can create focused lives for ourselves and choose to concentrate on the things we can control, like where and when to best spend our energy. By listening to our bodies and minds, we will find infinite ways to work smarter, not harder, and reclaim some of the productivity we may have lost.

Chapter 3: Personal Development

Today, one of the most popular life areas of goal setting is personal development or self-improvement. Many books, seminars, podcasts, or newspaper articles target you with the promise of a miraculously changed life if you follow just "three simple hacks." This sounds amazing because, let's be honest, we like simple fixes. We'd love to think that reading a book or listening to a seminar is enough to make us a better person and reach our optimal level of success.

What books usually don't tell you is this: The final aim of all self-development and improvement is to get to a point where you no longer need it. Let's say your wish is to become more attentive with others. The peak of this wish is to reach a level where you no longer have to concentrate about how to be more attentive.

The point of seeking happiness is to finally arrive at a place where you no longer have to seek it.

So in a paradoxical way, the aim of personal development is to slowly march toward a conceptual finish line where you no longer try to do it.

I'm sorry. This may sound quite discouraging. Bear with me until I unfold the point behind my lines above. We set lots of goals to please our environment, family, boss, our dog who is misbehaving by overtaking the alpha position in the house, etc. As we saw in the introduction, sticking to goals is not even the best use of our energy and willpower. Building strong habits is much more important and rewarding in the long-term. Goal setting helps you find the direction of improvement.

Before setting any kind of self-improvement goal, one should carefully examine the motivations behind that goal. In other words, what is your *why*?

Self-improvement goals will leave a bitter taste in your mouth, and trick a lot of money out of your pocket, if you pursue them for the wrong reasons. Why? Because you'll never reach that paradoxical line of not needing to practice your goal anymore. Sadly, the self-help industry is built around this hope — that you'll need to buy another book eventually, upgrade yourself to the royal/VIP-issimo package and a weekend in the Maldives for four figures to get the exclusive deal needed to fix whatever you need to fix. You'll chant mantras with two thousand other people, then go home charged with positivity just to sink back to your regular life after a week — two grand skinnier — thinking something's wrong with you. Because it must be. If a two-thousand-dollar luxury training couldn't fix you, there must be something wrong with you after all.

Now that I dragged your motivation to absolute rock bottom, let me tell you something good. There are ways to do self-improvement right. And you don't even have to sacrifice your emergency fund for it. However, it won't be quick. Personal development can't be pinned to a deadline. You can't possibly believe that if you color your Puppy Heaven hanging calendar with bright red on the 29th of December, you'll actually make a total personality change by then. Or learn a new language.

The first step in approaching self-improvement right is to accept that it will take time. A long time. Self-improvement is all about habit creation, not goal-chasing. There won't be a magical morning when you wake up with a total conviction that "Yes, now I'm changed." Change takes time, and you can usually observe it if you get a bit retrospective.

Think about the person you were five years ago. I bet you think that you're much wiser now than you were back in your twenties, or in your teenage years. That's how you measure change. Self-improvement in the present moment only serves you with a direction. All those tips and tricks and hacks are only worth as much as you practice them. Self-improvement is a marathon not a sprint.

The second step is to choose self-improvement for the right reason. As you can see, it is rather a tedious, long road to achieve anything real and lasting in this field. It's not a "change your hair, change your life" thing. Finding your whys before committing to self-improvement goals, therefore, is essential. You really don't want to waste five or ten years of your life just to become a person who can impress a cranky boss, or a you're-never-good-enough mother. When you choose a personal development direction for the sake of others, you'll usually fail. Somewhere on the long road, you'll lose the motivation to persist because you don't really want what you're pursuing, you're just seeking love or approval. Proof that goals eat up your stamina quickly — especially if the goal in question is something you don't want.

When you fail at accomplishing that goal, you'll resent yourself. You'll feel like a loser who can't persist. So you buy a book on improving persistence. But you don't really want to improve your persistence. You just add it as an unwanted side goal to the main (unwanted) goal. And here you are, carrying two burdens now that just cloud each of your mornings.

Some people stumble onto self-help material because they feel like something is wrong with them. The trap is that if something advises you how to improve your life, it is also suggesting that there is something off with you the way you are.

Search your whys. I know it sounds a cliché, but if you don't want to make the change for your own sake, your motivation won't outlast the time the change requires. Derek Sivers, a thinker and ex-business owner, once said, "If something is not a 'hell yeah,' don't go for it."

You live only once, you know. As I grow dangerously close to my thirties, I feel this more than ever. Some readers might growl or chuckle now with a sapient, thoughtful Churchill face. *"Oh, the things I saw in my life, junior."* Fair enough, my dear senior. In this case, you can confirm or contradict what I am about to say.

I just came back from a long, workless trip of five weeks. Hey, I hadn't actually had a vacation in ten years or so. I needed it. What do people do when they suddenly have nothing to do just look at trees that are much greener than the ones at home, or when they are surrounded by unfamiliar tastes and smells and juicy, inviting fruits that don't even have an English name?

After they have eaten so much of these nameless fruits they can barely move, they think.

So I was thinking a lot, making those kind of self-improvement-related reflections I was talking about above. I summarized what I'd learned from my twenties. Ten years is a fair timeframe in which to track and analyze some changes one has gone through.

Fail. Often, gracefully or totally outrageously.

In my twenties, I was so busy building myself up, learning new skills, exploring my talents, and coming up with wild ideas on how to change the world that I never really realize what my greatest asset was: time.

If you are in your twenties when you read this, please know that this is the time to take risks, to fail big-time, to get up and try again and repeat the process. To cry, to laugh, to eat a lot of chocolate without getting cellulite all over your lower body. Make mistakes.

Make hasty decisions that turn your parents' hair gray. Go and travel. Visit countries you didn't know existed before. Team up with your friends and sign up for a League of Legends championship. Move to another city while trying to build your online empire. Have a passionate relationship with a Guatemalan singer. This is the time to do all the weird *dolce vita* stuff. Seriously. In the long-term, you have nothing to lose. If you look back in your thirties, you'll realize that there is little to no difference between you being a total basket case at the age of twenty-one or twenty-six.

Your twenties are the only period in your life when you're not bound by parental scolding and restrictions, and you're also free of things that hit you in adulthood like piled up debts, kids, mortgages, and so on. Now is the time when you can and should make mistakes, experience hapless failures, and endure heartbreaks. These mistakes are invaluable life lessons that set you up for a better life in the future. They are the learning curves that prevent you from becoming a frustrated, depressed person whose everyday life consists of regrets and resentment. Mistakes, failure, and pain ultimately make you a better person.

If you're my senior and you now think you didn't do any of these in your twenties and the idea of having a passionate relationship with a Guatemalan singer appeals to you, you still can do it. It is never too late. However, time is your friend to a certain point. After that, it becomes your enemy. Some mistakes have the lowest cost in your early years.

Optimum life is just a fantasy. There will be no point in life where everything clicks into place like a puzzle, after which things will go smoothly. Each decade of life has its own problems, struggles, challenges, and wonders. Of course, there are habits and lifestyles that are better, healthier, and calmer than others. Talking with clients, friends, and random strangers older than me, we concluded that on the expanded picture of reviewing a decade, one thing really matters: Don't ruin the important things.

There are a limited number of things that really matter in life: your health, your closest relationships, and your financial security. And when I say health, I don't mean those two extra pounds. When I say good relationships, I don't mean that there will never be misunderstandings between you. When I say financial security, it's not about having millions in savings. I talk about those little nothings in life that we take for granted.

All the rest — even in self-improvement — provides only temporary satisfaction. The feeling of growth, the rush of positivity, and the awareness boost are just little tiles that make up the big picture. Therefore, if you mess up your daily to-do list a few times, it won't make you a worse person on the long run. Doing everything by the book in self-improvement won't necessarily make you a better one. Just because you feel like you're moving forward by completing a seminar doesn't mean you actually are.

Look back on the past ten years of your life. What do you think you've changed for the better in that period? What changed for the worse? Was there anything you tried to change, but you didn't succeed? Does it really matter? What were the habits that helped you the most? Was it worth making all the effort for a change in the past ten years? Or five? Or even one?

Who would you like to be in the next ten years? Imagine yourself ten years from today. Do the same retrospection as you are now on your imaginary next ten years. I would strongly suggest you to take a piece of paper, or a clean Word file, and write down everything you're thinking right now about how you imagine your next ten years will go. Put onto paper what you'd like to stay the same and what you'd like to change, not only about yourself, but also your surroundings. Would you like a new house? A larger bank account? A better husband? Children? More friends? Less friends? To write a book? What new things do you want to learn? New languages, new subjects? Microbiology? How many books do you want to read? What good habits do you want to have?

When you're done with this exercise, imagine yourself being ten years older. Who do you want to be? What skills or personality would you like to have by then? Center yourself in this plan. Don't try to become someone for others' sake. This exercise is about you and you only.

Save this script. Put it somewhere safe — in the drawer next to your birth certificate and passport, or in Dropbox. Take it out each year around the same time. Read it and contemplate how much closer you've gotten to the picture you've described. If something changed about your expectations, write it down on a different paper with a date and clip it to the original document. Don't discard the original, even if the change is as great as first wishing to become a hedge fund manager, then wanting to go and braid bracelets in Uruguay. Just see how much you and your wishes change in a decade's time. Also, when you cross that five-year or ten-year milestone, you'll be surprised at how many things you wished for became a reality.

You'll see that petty nonsense really just hurts in the moment. And in a ten-year perspective, even a four-month period seems like a moment. We change, our plans change, and that's why it is useless and dangerous to cast in iron any plan for the future. That's the beauty of life. You never know what the future will bring. Don't be like my friend who had her bushy brows totally eradicated to replace them with those creepy tattooed ones just because it was the fashion in the early 2000s, and now she's raging because bushy brows have become fashionable.

Don't mess up the big things. The irreversible things. The rest will be okay. As for self-improvement, the only real benefit of it is if one day you'll no longer need it, just like getting over the flu. Self-help is the lemon-honey-ginger tea. Drink it while you need it, and then drink your regular green banana smoothie.

Improvement is not always easy in the moment, though. I don't want to sell you snake oil by suggesting that you just hold on ten years, all will be good after that. I've read a splendid story on the process of self-formation. The author, Arsenie Boca, was a Romanian priest. His approach is religious, but the concept itself is so universal that everybody could relate with its figurative meaning.

The story is about a teacup. In the beginning, it was a lump of red clay. Then its master took the clay, hit it hard, kneaded it repeatedly, and the teacup-to-be cried out: *Stop hitting me, it hurts*. The master kindly replied: *Not yet*.

The clay was placed on a wheel and spun, and the master started to shape it. The teacup felt dizzy, sick, and like it'd had enough. Still the master replied with the same answer to its desperate entreaty: *Not yet.*

When the teacup became a cup in shape, it was put in the oven. It was incredibly hot; the cup cried. When it was taken out of the oven, the teacup thought finally it was over. It was the appropriate form now. It could relax, cool down, and never feel pain again.

But then the master started painting it, coloring beautiful figures and shapes on it. The cup, however, found the fumes and smell of the paint to be suffocating. The oven phase came again, but this time it was twice as hot and the cup felt it would die. It asked its master again. It insisted and screamed and cried. The cup was convinced that it would not survive. It was ready to quit.

The master took it out of the oven. *Take a look at you now*, he said. The teacup was impressed. It was a beautiful masterpiece, an exquisite item, a wonderful creation. The master added:

"I know it hurt, but if you had not been hit, spun, baked, if I had left you alone, you'd be dry. I know you were dizzy when I spun you on the wheel, but if I had stopped you would have crumbled. I know it hurt and it was hot and uncomfortable in the oven, but I had to put you there or you would have cracked. I know it didn't smell good when I brushed and stained you all over, but if I hadn't you'd never have hardened. You wouldn't have that glow in your life. If I had not put you into the oven for the second time, you would not have survived long."

It doesn't matter if you perceive the master in this story as God, destiny, or your own will, the message is the same: To become a better person, you must go through many layers of challenge and hardship. They shape you, toughen you up, and make sense later. I bet you had a heartbreak, a failure, or endured agony which at the moment you considered the worst that has happened to you, and years later, the best.

Do you have personal development goals? Do you know what habits you need to acquire to reach your goals?

Here is my last secret in that vein: You don't need to accomplish everything at once. This is difficult to digest, since we are conditioned to have a result-oriented focus. We learn it at school. If you do this, you get that score. If you do this better, you get a better score. If you don't do it, you get an F and all the kids will think that — based on your grades — you're dumb. This is the equation of school.

Later in life, however, things are not so linear and action-result based. It is important to have goals, to dream about them, because it gives life meaning. It gives you something to fight for. But achieving them is actually of no great importance. I hope I shocked you once more with my unpopular opinion.

Since my early twenties, I have been a big goal-setter. I sat down fairly often, penning a list of goals I wanted to accomplish. Some stuck with me longer than others. Looking back, I can say that I accomplished some of these goals. Some goals are still works in progress. But many of them became irrelevant, outdated, and I've done nothing about them. In the long run, I adopted some habits like consistency in work and learning something new each day that helps me get closer to some of my personal development goals. But there are goals I know I won't achieve.

I'm very satisfied, though. Even with the goals I never accomplished. They were good indicators of the things I only thought I wanted, but not really. I learned what had no real importance in my life. Surely, the goals I accomplished make me happy and proud and the person I'm today.

My conclusion about having personal development goals — or any kind of goal, for that matter — is important for the reason to get ourselves in motion. Achieving them is often beside the point. Through a natural process of selection, the really important ones will stick and the rest will be a sign of what we shouldn't consume our lives with. The learning curve is the learning curve.

Chapter 4: Relationship Goals

The main types of human relationships are: romantic, friendly, casual, family, and professional, according to the *Encyclopedia of Human Relationships*. As adults, we encounter all these five types in our lives.

Romantic relationships and family relationships are the most important ones in our lives. Romantic ones can be the most rewarding, but also the most troublesome.

Friendships are also essential in people's lives. We are social beings and need others to share opinions, ideas, and events with. Each of us must have a friend who is the only one we can talk a particular topic with. For example, one of my best friends is a total spirituality junkie — a very smart one. I can talk about anything with him that is soul-related. I have another good friend with whom I can talk about computer games all day long. With another friend, we can talk about nothing for hours, laughing like brainless cows. But if I changed the topics of discussion among these three friends, the conversations would become odd and dull.

Our friends have a great influence over us, since we care about their opinions. Therefore, it is crucial to surround ourselves with the right kind of people. Right, by the way, has only one characteristic: A person is right whom we like to be around, and who makes us a better version of ourselves. It has nothing to do with education, money, or other earthly values.

Good professional relationships can help us improve our skills and achieve our career goals and ambitions. The right connections increase our chances of getting promoted. Professional relations are valuable assets when we try to access alternative career opportunities.

Our casual relationships consist of interactions with everybody else who is not included in the other four groups mentioned above. These people don't have a real impact on our lives. If they say something positive, we acknowledge it with a good feeling and we move on. But sometimes, if we allow it, they can affect us negatively. All of us have met an unhappy salesperson, a grumpy doctor, a smile-shy driver, and so on. What they think or say doesn't impact our lives in the long run. If we let them inside our heads and hearts, they can ruin our entire day with a malicious comment.

Briefly, these five categories summarize all the human relationships we have. Each has their place and value in our lives. Here I'll focus on the relationship group that rises the most questions: romantic relationships. After all, our spouse is the person with whom we spend the most time.

Most of our lives... This sounds oddly Disney romantic on one hand and scary as hell on the other. It is almost stupid not to ask yourself from time to time, "What am I doing?" or "Where is this heading?" or "Am I with the right partner?" Some silly female magazines like to instill in you a fear of doubt. I think doubt is healthy, to a certain degree. It keeps your relationship in motion; it doesn't let you get too comfortable, and thus ruin everything. As long as you don't doubt the relationship and the person you're with as a whole long-term, a little self-questioning can do magic.

What do I mean? Let's imagine a scenario where you are sure that your partner will love you no matter what. Before it gets to your conscious mind, you leave behind all those little quirks he or she fell in love with you over and you become a cheeseburger-eating, Diet Coke-burping, oily-haired, never-on-time monster because "he or she loves me anyway." Since these changes happen gradually in your subconscious mind, you won't understand why your partner becomes more distant and dissatisfied. You find it unfair, so you yell at him while scratching your backside. "What the heck? I thought you loved me no matter what." He probably doesn't want to tell you that your behavior is disgusting, so he lies.

The lies escalate, and you become less and less motivated to make an effort. "If he doesn't like it, he can leave," you think. One fine day, he indeed leaves. And you are overwhelmed with pain. But what can you do? You have to get out on the dating market once more. So you buy a gym membership and a Sweat with Kayla app just to make sure. You take on a diet, a full-body waxing, some new stuff — just to show the jerk what he lost. In a few months, you'll become your best self again and trap another guy without even considering what went wrong in the previous round.

You see, the problem is not that the relationship ended. Not all relationships last. In the situation above, there were multiple problems — lack of communication, lack of honesty, and superficial reasons for staying together. But the very first mistake was made when one person took the relationship for granted.

Taking a relationship for granted is like thinking that you reached the maximum level of a skill. It stops you from improvement because you think there is nothing for you to improve anymore. You become comfortable. If you're comfortable, you won't put an effort into the relationship. It will become predictable and dull. People like feeling important, especially to their significant others. If they don't feel important, sooner or later will start seeking importance in other matters: their job, in sports, or in another person.

Not taking one's relationship for granted doesn't mean that you have to maintain the status quo of the beginning of the relationship. Stuff doesn't stay the same, especially if you see a long-term future together. You will both change and grow in unpredictable and unexpected ways. Be ready to embrace these changes while you're not taking the other person for granted.

Talking to multiple couples who have been together for ten, twenty, or even thirty years, I've learned that one of the most important long-term relationship goals is to accept the changes of the other one. Sometimes a twenty-year-long relationship lasts or fails on the couple's readiness to be able to embrace the changes of the partner.

Decades are a long time. Wishing for someone to stay the same for twenty years is not only unrealistic, but also unfair. Just think about how much you've changed in the past five years. The other person also changes. One day you'll realize that you're waking up next to a different person than you did ten years ago. Your relationship will depend on your ability to be able to fall for this new person, too. And vice versa.

However, the foundation of a relationship is not acceptance. Not even love — sorry, Disney. It is respect.

If there is a solid bedrock of respect in the relationship, it is almost a given that you'd wish for your partner to change for the better and grow. If there is respect, you're not afraid to speak up if you feel he or she changes in a bad direction, either. If there is respect on their side, they will accept your remark because they know you mean well. If mutual respect is given, then it is just a matter of communication when it comes to drifting over the occasional changes a person goes through. What matters is to be aware of the changes of your partner, and don't cease to respect and accept these changes.

Don't get me wrong. These changes are not things like, "Maria was a gourmet wine drinker, but now she brings a Heineken home and each evening she gulps it." The changes I'm talking about here are those real deal breaker changes, like moving to another country because of a change of worldview, having an old parent who suddenly needs a lot of financial support, the death of a child, becoming a badass feminist when you, or they, were once a model housewife. These kinds of changes.

The only force that carries couples through these difficulties is mutual respect. Changes don't happen overnight, and by the time they do, love won't be that burning, passionate butterfly maze it was in the first year, so you can't really rely on it. Be aware that the person you commit to today won't be the same person in ten years.

This idea brings us to another important relationship point: Choose your partner for the right reasons.

There is a blurred line between what's right or wrong in most cases. But let's see a few examples of the definitely wrong reasons to commit to someone:

- Pressure from family. I mean, we're not living in the 1500s anymore. I know in some cultures it is still popular for the family to choose the future husband or wife for their kids, and I don't mean to be disrespectful to them. However, in the age where the Japanese princess renounces her royalty status just to get married to a "commoner," you as an individual can also choose to take charge of your fate. It may have a price; make sure you're willing to pay it.

If you don't follow the arranged marriage culture, maybe you've just had enough of your mom tormenting you with "marrying Lucy, who's such a nice girl." Don't give in and marry her just to make your mom shut up. Or do it and know that you'll make some lawyer very happy and rich in the next one to five years.

- Don't settle for the first person who comes along after a long wait of getting in a relationship. Many people struggle to find a partner. Not the right partner, but just a partner. So when they do, they settle without a second thought. They engage in many unhealthy compromises and tie the knot before their partner vanishes.

This kind of marriage stands on quicksand usually, because at least one member of the relationship doesn't even know how to be in a relationship. Someone who settles for the first person out of fear of remaining single forever ("a loser") probably has a low self-esteem, which will backfire sooner or later.

- Marrying young, hopelessly in love, like Romeo and Juliet. Well, we know how that story went. A three-day relationship between a thirteen- and seventeen-year-old caused six deaths — including their own.

- Marrying because you're a good match. Maybe you look equally good — or bad — together physically, or financially. Staying together for the image, to make the community envious, or other bourgeois BS, is a bad idea.

- Choosing someone to "fix" or "heal" yourself. The aim to use the love of someone else to lick your wounds and ease your emotional distress is wrong. Not just for the other person, but for you too. This kind of behavior leads to codependence, which won't heal you. It just generates an unhealthy and harmful dynamic in the relationship. It's not healing, just a silent agreement to use love as an excuse to avoid facing deeper problems.

Now that we went through some bad reasons, let's look at the good reasons for marriage. There is no right answer that guarantees you a successful marriage, because almost all the superficial and non-superficial reasons you choose to marry someone will change or go away after a while.

There are some strong pillars that reduce the risk of a failed relationship. These pillars, however, shouldn't be taken for granted. They should be worked on over the course of your lives. What a long-lasting relationship needs from the first moment is a profound admiration and respect for each other. Without these two things, everything else will unravel with time.

So where is love in the equation of choosing a partner? Love is the part where you divide each element of the equation with one — it's neutral.

If you both are healthy individuals, love will help, bring joy, and laughter. If you're not whole as a person, love will bring doubt, bitter tears, and pain. Love is the extra, but never enough to sustain a relationship by itself.

The next cornerstone to make a relationship work is a counterintuitive one. Expect disasters, fights, and disagreements. They will come. So what do you do when they occur?

"Don't wish for less problems, wish for more skills." This is a quote from Jim Rohn. In this case it means learn how to fight and get to the bottom of problems. I must emphasize the importance of respect again. No matter how well you communicate, how kind and disciplined you are with your criticizing words, in some cases it won't be enough. Some conflicts can't be avoided. Some criticism will always be painful, no matter how nicely it's packaged. Still, if you trust the good intentions of the other person, if you hold each other in high esteem, if you believe that he or she didn't mean to harm you intentionally, the problem will be solved at the end of the day.

To assume the best of the other person requires respect and trust. Without those things, you will doubt each other's intentions. You'll be suspicious and defensive. You or your partner will think that you can't tell your honest opinion because you fear the consequences. This is the first sign of cracks in the foundation.

John Gottman is an amazing psychologist and relationship researcher. He's spent his last three decades meeting and analyzing married couples, trying to decipher what the key things that make a marriage (or relationship) work are and what pulls people apart. If you read any book on the topic, chances are that his work has been referred to in the text. What makes Gottman's research so unique?

When he meets a couple, instead of telling them to say good things about each other, he asks them to have a fight. They are supposed to choose a problem they have and talk about it in front of cameras. After the couple leaves, Gottman analyses the recording and can predict with almost flawless accuracy whether the couple will split or not. What do you think he sees on those videos? What do you think he is basing his prediction on?

It is not the fury or passion people fight with each other. It is not the lack of fight, either. Every couple fights, even if they never raise their voice or don't drop f-bombs all over.

Based on his more-than-a-quarter-of-a-century experience, he broke down four typical fight patterns that he calls "the four horsemen" that usually lead to divorce.

These are:

- Criticism of one's character. For example, "you are so dumb" instead of "what you did was not smart."
- Contempt: bringing down your partner with words, making them feel inferior, less valuable as a person.
- Defensiveness: making excuses all the time, trying to throw the blame back to the other person. Not taking responsibility for your own actions and mistakes, but rather trying to escape fault by incriminating the other.

- Stonewalling: basically walking away from a problem, not listening to your partner, avoiding problem solving.

Gottman carefully analyzed the presence of these four horsemen in any fight he listened to. Science and the feedback of couples, not to mention the accuracy of his predictions, back up what he's preaching.

Don't patronize, name-call, or belittle your partner. Contempt is the leading reason for separation in a couple.

Another tip to have a constructive fight is to avoid bringing the ghost of previous fights into the present one. A fight usually is complicated enough by itself. Bringing other elements into it will just make it harder to solve and people twice as mad and desperate.

If the conversation takes an overly emotional angle, better take a break. Go make tea, watch a YouTube cat video, or go for a walk. Don't insist on solving the issue here and now because "I don't want to come back and think about this stuff again later." Go take a cold shower or walk around your neighborhood. Think through what you're about to say and imagine how you would react if you got that criticism in your face. Try to rephrase it into something you'd be able to digest.

Don't forget that being "right" is beside the point. Striving to be right at all costs can inflict a lot of damage. It can make the other party feel unheard and disrespected. Making your partner feel unloved is a high price to pay for your righteousness. Make sure you know what your goal is: to solve the problem or to prove you're right. In a relationship, an argument is hardly ever black and white anyway. You might think you're right, but so may your spouse. If both of you position proving the other wrong to be the goal of the fight, a hard negotiation will form, making the issue impossible to be solved. It will create resentment and lead to contempt, stonewalling, and other deal breakers. Don't be a fatalist in a fight.

Speaking of fatalism, the other extreme is when people don't have a fight. Like, ever. We all know at least one couple who take pride in never fighting. Also, this couple just split last week, and your friend from the couple complains to you ever since about all the things he never said to his ex.

No relationship book has ever been written without emphasizing the importance of good communication. However, they often fail to explain what this vague term means more precisely. When I was younger, I used to think that "good communication" equaled nice communication. I thought as long as I was composed and kind, and I didn't speak loudly or use swear words, the communication was good. And if the problem persisted, that was not my fault. It was "that stupid monkey who messed it up again because he never listens." Eek, contempt — I'm not together anymore with the ape in question. It's little wonder why.

So, what is good communication? Firstly, it's nothing more than being okay with having uncomfortable talks. Engaging in fights, if needed. Not sugarcoating the ugly, but getting your feelings out as they are. Once they are out, assume the best of the other person (respect, you remember) and know that these words are not targeted to hurt you, but to solve an issue.

At the end of the day, the cliché remains true: There is no problem that can't be solved when both parties are dedicated to solving it for the sake of the relationship.

This leads to another important aspect of a good relationship — becoming good at forgiving. Good fighting skills require good forgiving skills.

How to be a better forgiver? Most importantly, try not to stay in a post-argument frenzy for days. When a fight is over, it's over. Make this a relationship goal. It doesn't matter who was right or wrong, naughty or nice — when the fight is done, you won't bring it back to the present. Of course, to be able to do this, the fight has to be effective and the agreement to close it must be honestly mutual. This rule can be applied to small issues like, "Why didn't you bring the trash out?" to larger ones such as, "Why did you cheat on me?" The healing time is different, but once you decide to forgive, forgive.

Keep punishments out of the picture. Don't think, or worse, demand that your spouse owes you something just because the kitchen smells like garbage for two days. Avoid being the unquestionable expert — "I know how to manage the household finances better, so back off." Relationships are not a zero-sum game. Don't "I bought you the watch you wanted for Christmas, but you didn't get me the massage chair" your partner. There is no scoreboard you need to equalize at the end of the month.

If you feel you give much more than you get long-term, open a discussion about it in civilized manner. Don't bully, manipulate, or blackmail the other without telling them what your problem is. Make sure whatever you give, you give it unconditionally. Without expecting anything in return. That's what love is all about.

Separate intentions from the behavior. It is much easier to forgive this way. Your partner may have screwed it up, but know that he was doing the best he could at the moment. He is not a bad person because involuntarily he struck a sensitive nerve in you. He didn't say those words because he wanted to break up with you in such a roundabout manner. He's not criticizing you because he loves someone else secretly. If you try to be objective, you'll see the issue for what it is — the way a good person tries his best to talk about something that presses his mind. You know him better than to assume the worst. You're with him because he is good.

If you can't bring yourself to think all these things when your partner messes up, the trust and respect is seriously damaged in your relationship. Then the issue is not the present issue, but something deeper and harder to fix. You'll need a lot of patience and dedication and communication to overcome such a deep distrust.

What relationship goals do you have? Do you wish for a healthy romantic relationship? Make sure to keep your wishes from turning into expectations. Love has no conditions, but relationships do. These conditions are, however, not expectations. In relationships, both parties should willingly, unselfishly uphold values like respect, honesty, caring, loyalty, compassion, attention, and supporting the other to become the best version of themselves. Where there is this kind of love, there is no claim and no addiction.

In a good romantic relationship, both parties can be themselves. They take pleasure in the other person's individuality, looks, and attitude on life. They are happy for each other. They are companions.

The thoughts mentioned above apply to friendships too. Except the romantic factor, of course. Help your friends, advise them if they ask you to, but do not force your expectations upon them. Don't outsmart them. Try to stay neutral. There are so many ways you can make your point without offending the other person. For example, instead of saying the person was wrong, say something like:

"I accept that you think that way. You may be right. Please tell me more about your viewpoint..."

In this way, you can go to "battle" with flowers and not arrows. Also, you won't make the other person defensive. You said you agreed, so they can't counterattack you with an opposing opinion. By showing good faith and a willingness to listen to the other's opinion, she will be more inclined to listen and consider yours. Understand first, be understood after.

When engaging in an argument, remember that there is no full victory. You always lose something. You may lose the opportunity to prove yourself right. Or you may win the argument, but lose your argument partner's good will. It doesn't matter who this person is — a family member, your spouse, or somebody you just met.

My final thoughts on relationship goals are the following:

- You can get over any hardship. But make sure in the meantime, none of you gets destroyed physically, emotionally, spiritually, or financially.
- Write love letters to each other. Nope, not emails. Actual letters.
- Don't be ashamed of who you are in front of your intimate partner. Do not shame your partner either for what makes him or her happy.
- Have a discussion at least yearly about the good things, changes, and problems

over the last year. Also talk about where do you see your lives as individuals and as a couple drifting in the next year. Discuss how you could manage the existing problems better, and how could you support each other's endeavors.

- Have a life as an individual, but share it through conversation with your partner.

- Don't forget about each other even when the kids arrive. They are the fruit of your love. Don't let that love die. Your spouse comes first.

- Welcome each other's growth. Be the first one who supports the growth, not the one who tries to repress it.

- Don't assume the other party will hold the relationship together. Rather, assume it is your task. If both of you do this, the relationship will grow and survive.

- Keep your dirty laundry at home. Don't complain about your love to other people — especially not to seek some one-sided reinforcement for your current resentment. Do you want to legitimize your anger, or solve the problem?

- Make love even when you aren't in the mood for it.
- Trust each other.
- Be transparent. Don't do anything that you wouldn't tell your spouse.
- Be proud of each other.
- Disagree with respect. Be ready to change and to accept. Trust that your partner will do the same.
- Go to counseling as prevention, not as a solution. Build up a good structure for your relationship with a professional.

Chapter 5: Health

You only have one body. Look after it! By having effective health habits which you can maintain and practice daily, your life span and quality of life will rise significantly.

Health and well-being come from a mixture of multiple lifestyle factors. Just by eating healthy, you won't become bulletproof. Lifestyle improvement activities are all inter-linked. To improve one aspect of your health, you need to focus on your overall health balance.

What are the main aspects of healthy lifestyle?

- Nutrition
- Exercising
- Optimal weight
- Spiritual balance

What's your health goal?

- How many years do you want to live in good health?
- Maybe you want to become a triathlete at the age of fifty?
- Or maybe you want to run a marathon every year?
- Would you like to eat healthier?

It is never too late to start living a healthy lifestyle, but the sooner, the better. Even if you are only twenty and fit as a fiddle now, you will not stay that way forever. I am closer to thirty than twenty, and I can see some minor changes in my body already. The springy flesh disappears after twenty-six if there is nothing there to hold it. Some people realize they've missed being sporty and the time when exercise was easier.

Do you want to lose weight?

The best thing you can do is to get clear about what your purpose is with a diet. Are you hoping for a healthy lifestyle or losing weight? If the latter, you might want to consider some aspects before choosing your weight loss diet.

The best thing you can do is to consult a registered dietitian. Ask for help to come up with a plan tailored to your needs. Take with you a three-day summary of what you usually eat so the dietitian can create a personalized plan that meets your nutritional needs, but also your lifestyle.

The most important aspect of any diet you should take into consideration is your ability to keep it. Most experts agree that it doesn't matter how rigorously researched and complex a diet is; if it doesn't fit your lifestyle, eating habits, or religious beliefs, chances are high that you'll give up on it.

"It doesn't matter how scientifically sound the program is (and many are not), how fast they work (you will regain as fast as you lost), or even how many people have tried it before. What matters is whether you can do what they say forever — not whether you should, but whether you can." says Michelle May, MD, author of *Am I Hungry?* for WebMD.

"Most people go on and off fad diets and fall into the yo-yo syndrome of dropping weight, followed by gaining weight. "The consequence is you lower your metabolism and end up at a heavier weight than when you started," states a professor of nutrition at the University of North Florida.

When choosing a diet, you should consider whether it matches your way of eating. For example, consider the frequency of your meals, what you eat on the go, business dinners, family-friendly approach, etc. Can you cook the meals at home? How much time does it require? Can you fit it in your budget? Can you meet the level of exercise needed? Can you live on this diet forever? Can you still eat your favorite foods occasionally?

These are very important questions to answer to predict your diet's sustainability. Take the time to answer them before you choose one by yourself, or agree upon one with your dietitian.

I chose a simple, easy to follow program that didn't steer me wrong. I am fit, healthy, and feel energized. I'll tell you about my daily health routine later, but first let me tell you what helped me decide.

If you choose to trust somebody as a health advisor, check how this person thinks, eats, and trains. Does he follow his own advice?

Does her routine match your goals? (For instance, you shouldn't do what a bodybuilder does unless your goal is to be a world-class bodybuilder.)

Can you implement these routines in your life?

Set realistic expectations. If you didn't get any exercise for years, it would be silly to pledge to run five miles the next day. You probably won't even get your sneakers on. But if you set a goal of walking a mile the first day, this may be achievable. Be patient. Improve your own limits slowly but surely.

The main point of starting small is to become proud of yourself, to feel a glimpse of success. If you promise yourself something unrealistic that you know you won't achieve in the near future, the bitter taste of self-resentment will take over. That's quite the opposite outcome. If it's better for you, set deadlines — *in four months, I will run five miles*. Then focus your energy to do it. Break the five miles into weekly and daily targets. Start with 300 feet, 500 feet, then by the end of the first week, try to reach a one-mile jogging target. And so on.

It doesn't really matter what you do, just do it. In the beginning, it will not be easy.

A healthy lifestyle isn't only about keeping your body, your brain, and your stomach in shape. Do not forget about another core part of your being that needs to be nurtured just as much: your soul. I could also call it your spirit, mood, wellbeing, and so on. Your brain guides your soul, but just reading or doing crosswords doesn't touch this part of your spirit. This very part of your mind is responsible for your joy or sorrow.

If your give your soul things that make it happy, you'll feel energized. If you don't pay attention to your soul, or you cause yourself pain, you'll feel miserable, and it is an utterly unhealthy state to be in.

For example, some people are fit both physically and mentally, and eat healthily. Still, they seem blue and under the weather all the time. Even though they seem to be the perfect human specimen, they catch colds easier than others and feel they lack energy. Why? Because their soul is neglected.

Having healthy meals, exercises, and readings is critical to keep your body healthy, but they aren't everything. Food for your soul is just as important. Without a happy soul, there is this inexplicable phenomenon with people that they let their guards down — subconsciously — and get tired easier. They will become more sensitive to illnesses, and in extreme cases, can become depressed.

On the other side, it has been proven through research that those people who suffer from a grave illness but have very strong spirit (they still have a lot of people, activities, and other motivations to nurture their soul with) tend to recover in a higher percentage, or live much longer than expected.

How can you nurture your soul? By practicing the values dearest to you. What are your core values? Love? Quality time with family and friends? Helping people in need? Stroking your cat? Spending some quality "me time"? Collect at least five experiences that hold special value for you and start practicing them more often. Wake up earlier every second day to prepare a coffee for your spouse. Call your mother more often. Get your cat a special meal. Usually the things that make us the happiest involve making someone else happy.

Chapter 6: Money Management

Let's pretend for a moment that you just graduated college and have decided that you want to become rich. That's a fair goal to have, right? If you were rich, you could get rid of all the burdens you have — like paying off your debts, switching to a health-conscious lifestyle, or just be the next baller of the neighborhood and organize parties at your house with a pool, where you park your Lamborghini and drink imported prosecco from Tuscany.

Now, that you have everything that matters laid out, you just need to find a way to create that wealth. Most people think that wealth creation works like this: You make your first thousand — more or less easily. Sweating bullets, you work yourself up to $10k a month. In a few years of crazy labor, you'll have some savings in your account, but you'll still live in a crappy little apartment in the cheap side of the town. What to do to bring this to the next level? How will you get that Lamborghini under your butt in this phase? "Whatever," you think, and settle on buying a gigantic TV, an upgraded couch, and a cat instead, letting go of your grandiose dreams along with your savings.

This is a very typical way people handle their financial goals in their early years of work. And yes, you're right. Most of them are not rich. People who get rich eventually do things differently. In their case, the first hard-earned thousand bucks are invested in self-improvement that brings them to earn $10k per month. They invest that ten thousand as well in improving their skills and assets that will bring them to a hundred thousand a month. In the big picture, money makes more money and will open the doors of pool parties where they can ball around like Jordan Belford.

This is the basic difference between people. Some look at money as something they can spend — in other words, they have a spending mindset. Other people look at money as something they can invest to make more money. This mindset is called the saving mindset.

Most people get off track at their job choices because they are obsessed with the New Age craze of finding your passion. True, having a miserable job will leave its mark on your other life areas. It will lead to a tense family life and your free time will be filled with anxiety. The money you earn will make you feel you're in constant scarcity because you'll believe that the price you pay for earning it is too high, so whenever you spend it, you feel a painful knot in your stomach. Thus, you won't be able to enjoy anything you buy on that money. Also, if your job isn't offering the chance for personal achievements, growth, or entertainment, it will make you tired and disappointed.

If your job is so very bad, then change careers. Do something less bad. But even then, who says you can always find a way to make money doing only what you love? Since when are people so convinced that having a good job means loving each second of it? I consider myself extremely lucky that I can live off writing — I have flexibility, freedom of artistic expression, yet even I hate my job from time to time.

What to do then? What kind of job should one settle on?

Cal Newport, the author of *So Good They Can't Ignore You*, gives a solid answer to these questions. He states you shouldn't focus on following your passion, finding your true calling, or self-actualization. This way of thinking only gets you lost in the maze of unrealistic expectations and disappointment. Again, no job will be amazing 100% of the time. Not even 80%. Mr. Newport warns that looking for passion, purpose, or calling can steal precious time from people, can deter focus from things that really matter, and leads to procrastination. People think that their passion is an intrinsic and unchanging gift inside of them. However, they won't find anything inside because that's not where a true feeling of passion comes from.

Passion and purpose are the consequence of expertise and experience. Commit to getting great at something, master that knowledge, do great work, and savor the burning passion and contentment that follows.

Cal Newport says the timeline of passion is reversed from what most people think. First, settle on any kind of work you don't hate doing, but do have a slight interest in. Then master this work. Don't slow down until you've become valuable in your field, instead of looking for passion and purpose. The better you become, the more passionate you'll become in what you do. Why? Because you will know what you're doing, you'll fail less, and you'll earn more admiration (and money). Purpose and passion only follow the great career, not precede it. The author calls the long-term path to passion through excellence the "craftsman's path."

People who became great at a profession started with working on their craft every day. They didn't stop even if the time wasn't right, or they weren't in the mood. They had persistence, devotion, and hard work, even if they didn't feel passionate about it that day or month. Excuses about a far-from-ideal work environment or unrewarded work quality will keep you from mastering the craftsman's path. Stay resilient, keep working on your goal of getting better, and avoid making excuses as to why you don't do something.

It is not an easy path, and surely not a quick one. It will take you hundreds, even thousands, of hours of practice. But with time, you'll achieve mastery. This path is under your control. The key takeaway of the "craftsman's path" is to build rare and valuable skills, experience, earn a great career, and passion and purpose will come as a byproduct.

Another interesting concept the book presents is "career capital." It is not a new concept, generally speaking, but Mr. Newport attaches some unique attributes to this asset. He advises us to use our career capital that we grind together over the years to make the change we truly wish for. During our years of working on excellence we build expertise, connections, experience, and a good reputation.

What Mr. Newport highlights is not to forget how valuable this asset is. When we feel like we've had enough and want to make a career change, we should primarily "spend" the career capital we've earned the past few years of hard work, making sure not to lose it because of hasty decisions.

If we jump from our current field to a totally different field, we lose all the career capital we have collected. It's like being in a computer game. If we exit one faction and enter another, we'll lose our experience points, even our armor and ranking. We have to start from the beginning. The only thing remaining is our knowledge about the process of how to build up a good and strong character.

The author of *So Good They Can't Ignore You* tells us to not just quit and throw away all the career capital we have. It's better if we take the time to find a way to use the valuable knowledge we've built up to make the transition to another field.

The key takeaway of the idea of "career capital" is to use our connections, reputation, expertise, and knowledge to get into a higher position in the new field before leaving the old one. This way, the career capital is not wasted and you don't have to start the new work from scratch.

But let's be real for a moment. We, as a generation, have a very low tolerance for unpleasantness and discomfort. What is so bad about working a normal job with nice people and pursuing whatever you feel passionate about in your free time? The honest truth is every job will feel like a burden sometimes. There's no mysterious activity that you will never get bored of or stressed over. That's fairy dust. And what you experience, that's just life.

Each job-related question and argument can be broken down to one subject (beyond self-realization), and this is money. This is a sensitive subject because many people associate their self-worth to how much money they make. Our worth in money, to a certain degree, will dictate our identity. Speaking in economic terms, our income shows a measurable valuation of our skills and worth on the market. No wonder most of us get a bit defensive and touchy when the infamous topic of finances comes up in a conversation.

What people forget is that money by itself doesn't hold any kind of value. What you can turn your money into is where the real value lies. And I'm not talking about the newest phone. Time has real value. Or knowledge. Or positive emotions like happiness, fulfillment, and love.

Money, therefore, is just to tool you can use to get more of these values.

Money doesn't define you as a person; however, what you spend your money on can. For example, if you spend your money on some quality time with your loved ones, making everyone happy, that shows you have admirable values. If you spend the same amount of money on the yacht of a Russian mobster, getting unknown girls drunk and smoking like it's the end of the world, you can still be a good person with shittier priorities.

Money is not the cause of happiness or unhappiness, or even wealth in your life; it's the effect. It is, however, the most obvious effect. As the example above shows, money is only a reflection of your values and priorities. If you have money and you spend it in a wasteful, or worse, harmful way, it won't make you rich.

This being said, there is an emotional side of money. If you think money is bad, money will leave your pocket. If you hate money, you'll lose it. Subconsciously, you'll drive yourself to spend it. The classic situation is when you get promoted: you get thirty percent more income and start spending. Then you're shocked that you didn't save more money than the previous month when you were making less. We don't want to keep something we think is bad, after all. If you think money is bad — instead of neutral — slowly you'll sabotage yourself into constant scarcity.

How do you prevent this? By changing your beliefs about money. Instead of giving money a bad name, attach it something good and enjoyable. Don't think about money as cause for pain, but rather as a tool you can exchange for something that really matters to you. That really makes you happy.

"The things you own end up owning you," said a very wise person. Just kidding, this quote comes from the movie *Fight Club.* Nevertheless, its message is just as truthful as if it was said by a triple Ph.D. Today we live in an epidemic called "more." We always feel the need to buy more things, earn more, look better, accumulate more... Today's materialism is a vicious psychological trap. We also sacrifice more to sustain our craving for more. We spend a lot from other values to possess valueless things. We sacrifice our time, often quality time with our loved ones.

You may think all this happens because of that filthy money. Because it poisoned your mind. Nope, my friend. Money has nothing to do with that. You poisoned it yourself. Money is neutral, a tool for exchange of "goods." You give your goods (skills, experience) to someone else (your boss) and you get money. Then you pay for other people's goods with money.

Whenever you buy something, you buy an experience — not just the tool itself. If you buy a motorcycle, you're buying the feeling of driving it, not only the metal monster. You also buy an identity — you're the dude with the Harley. The Harley is cool, thus you're cool. You're decorating your identity with fancy gadgets, and you pay for this sense of power and status as well. This doesn't mean you'll be happy with your motorbike and all the experience you bought with it. I just want to point out that whenever you exchange your money for something, you buy much more than the object.

This cycle is true in case of cheaper, more essential things like food. You're not only buying your hotdog, but also the peace of mind of not becoming hungry anytime soon. If you buy a ticket to Disneyland for your family, you're buying the possibility to bond, to deepen relationships, and create lifelong memories. When you buy a Hugo Boss suit, you buy status and an air of professionalism. When you buy a puppy, you buy the endless positive feelings that little creature will give you. I could go on with the examples, but they all break down to this one conclusion: Whenever you use your credit card, it's not about the things you purchase. Those objects are the vessel for something more spiritual, a feeling, an experience.

Our entire adult life is a loop of experiences. We work to earn the money — which usually seems like a bad experience — to exchange it later to good experiences.

There are four ways people sabotage their financial life. Each of these ways are emotionally destructive. They all stand in the way of a well-balanced financial life. Do you think you fall into one of the following categories?

1. The Scarcity Loop

People who've never had enough money don't know how to handle it. Any positive experience related to money is unknown for them. They earn the money as a negative experience — they grind and struggle to make ends meet. But they also spend the money as a negative experience, being constantly in terror of, "What if I won't have money tomorrow?" Their financial life is a never-ending loop of hell. They hate money, therefore they spend it (see the explanation above). But at the same time, they are terrified of running out of money. They face a cruel paradox.

2. The Ego Loop

People suffering in the ego loop are those you constantly feel inferior at their workplace. Their job is not rewarding, they don't feel appreciated, or worse, they feel like an insignificant loser. Since the negative experience to earn money is related to their perceived inferiority, they try to compensate for it by buying expensive status symbols. Their positive experience of spending money is intertwined with the negative

105

experience of earning it. Insecurity gives birth to the money, thus insecurity consumes it. People stuck in the ego loop spend their money quickly before they could get the chance to accumulate it.

3. The Stress Loop

Oh boy, there are those people who are always in a hurry, always busy, never able to snap out of work mode. They have to put up with a great deal of stress. The stress can come from two sources, whether they have a high-pressure job where they have a bigger responsibility than they can handle, or their stress is self-generated.

Whatever the cause, stress steals away most of their life. Therefore, whenever they can, they spend their money on stress-relief. They are stuck in the cycle of stress-accumulation and stress-relief without being able to save too much money in the meantime.

4. The Misery Loop

People stuck in this loop expose themselves to actual pain and misery to earn money. It can be physical (stunt, fakir, professional boxer) or emotional (abusive people at the workplace, selling one's body for money) misery. They exchange the experience of making money on pain relief more often than anybody else. When I say pain relief, I mean cigarettes, alcohol, drugs, and other temporary numbing tools.

To be able to properly enjoy the positive experiences related to money, you need to detach yourself from automatic compensation for the negative experiences. This is the first step. Acknowledge what kind of pain you feel as a direct consequence of your job. Is it fear of not having enough? Is it stress? Is it a feeling of inadequacy? Or pain in its truest meaning? Realize that if you don't change something, it's going to cost you a lot — and not just in monetary value.

Write down the pain you experience due to the experience of making money. What are you working for? What would you like to buy if you had unlimited resources? Why do you work? What's your main goal with money? Write everything you want to exchange your money for.

- How much income do you wish for?
- What properties and cars would you like?
- How much savings would you like to have?
- What standard of living do you want?
- What else would you like to do with your money? Gain knowledge? Help a family member in need?

Know what your true purpose is with the money you earn. Keep that in mind and remind yourself whenever you're about to spend your money on compensatory experiences.

The second step is to realize that true wealth isn't a heavy bank account, but when you are able to spend your money not simply to compensate for how you make it. True wealth is when you spend and earn your money as a positive experience.

The third step, the step of getting out of any of the four cycles above, is to stop using money as your definer of success. Stop making your paycheck a part of your identity. Stop thinking that your income equals your value as a person..

It sounds very simple, but as soon as you do it, magic will happen. You won't feel the need to spend your money on compensatory experiences. You'll also relieve yourself from any work-related stress: if you don't identify with your money, you won't feel inferior. If you don't position your income as your main definer, you won't be so stressed about making more and more. Money is just a tool of success, it doesn't equal success. You'll feel truly satisfied with your money when you let it go as a flag of success and you start using it as a leverage of success. Use it to get the values that are truly important.

Use your money to support your loved ones, to give birth to a long-cherished creative business, to make yourself healthier, and to become a better person.

Be grateful for what you have.

At least eighty percent of the world's population lives in poverty, scarcity, or debt. Many tell themselves that tomorrow they will get out of it, only to fall deeper into debt. Why? Because that tomorrow never comes. "The chains are too weak to be felt until they're too strong to be broken," said Warren Buffet.

Some say, "Oh, I don't want to be a billionaire." Just like when somebody starts to go to the gym, they say, "Oh, I don't want to be a bodybuilder." There is much more work behind that goal than just lifting weights a few times a week. The same is true with money — you can reach a comfortable level of wealth, but to become somebody who truly has a financial impact on society requires a lot of study, hard work, and resourcefulness.

Earning money is not only about making it a positive experience. It is also about working smarter — this will enhance the positive experience. But how does one work smarter?

You can trade your time for money, but that's not the smartest thing to do long-term. Or you can come up with ideas on how to become more productive. In my early twenties I had two jobs, and I kid you not, I worked twelve to sixteen hours a day — including Saturdays. In terms of income, I made okay money considering the Hungarian average, but I didn't have a life. I literally had eight hours to socialize, work out, and ultimately, to sleep.

Some people have well-paying jobs, but they are not happy. Others are artists, doing what they love, but they can't make ends meet. Both of them experience money-making as a negative process. Only a small group of people actually do what they love and make good money from it. The rest can be divided in three groups: the ones who make a lot, but hate what they do; those who love what they do, but make no money; and finally, those who hate what they do, and they don't even make money from it.

Derek Sivers, former musician, entrepreneur, philanthropist, and millionaire, in one of his articles on his website, www.sivers.org, offers the following solution to this problem:

Strive to have a well-paying job to have financial security, and also seriously pursue your passion, but for the sake of love, not money. Mr. Sivers says that the happiest people he knows are those who can balance their job and their passion.

"We all have a need for stability and adventure, certainty and uncertainty, money and expression. Too much stability, and you get bored. Not enough, and you're devastated. So keep the balance. Do something for love, and something for money."

Choosing a job that gives you a solid future is a mental choice, not a choice made with your heart. Have this stability in your life. You don't have to do this job your entire life. Do it until something better shows up.

If you feel that you have a passion for art, work on it seriously in your free time. Get better and feel the progress you make each week. Then try to sell it, get fans. It has never been so easy to self-promote your artwork as it is today. There is Amazon, Etsy, Alibaba, and many other platforms you can take advantage of.

Don't forget, you don't sell your passion for money, you do it for yourself because you love doing it, to start building up a positive experience that is work-related. Positive attitude changes the chemistry of the selling process. You won't be selling your artwork as someone who needs the money. *"You don't need to please the marketplace. No need to compromise your art, or value it based on others' opinions. You're just doing this for yourself — art for its own sake. And you're releasing it because that's one of the most rewarding parts, is important for self-identity, and gives you good feedback on how to improve."*

You can never know what will happen with your artwork out there. You may just sell it for the sake of learning to attach work to positive experiences. Take the positive charge your artwork generates in you to your money-making job.

Now you know what you need to do to experience work as a good thing. Are you an accountant who loves to paint? Bring an extra sheet of paper and doodle when you have a minute to spare. Strive to transform your work into a positive experience. It doesn't matter where you fish that experience out.

When I had my two jobs and no life, I wrote a book. I had zero background. Zero. No fans, nobody who knew who Zoe McKey was. I didn't even have native English language skills. I also had zero expectations with my book. I wrote it and published it. I had nothing to lose publishing it, but I loved writing it. I wrote my book secretly when I was working. I wrote the book on my spare Sunday. I wrote the book in those eight hours of freedom I had a day.

After a month, I published it, and the book made more than my day job. After two months, it made more than my two jobs together. After three months, I quit both of my jobs and I devoted myself to writing.

I'm not saying this will happen to everybody who dares trying. It won't. But you can never know. I, for sure, had all the odds against me.

If I may be so bold to suggest you a financial goal, it would be this:

Figure a way to transform your money-making experience into a positive one. Do whatever needs to be done to achieve this: change jobs, talk with your boss, start a side hustle, get a plant on your desk. Just do it. If the money-making experience is good, the money-spending experience will be good too. Don't expect your work to be easy. Find the beauty of hard-earned creation.

Chapter 7: Free Time

What do you want to do? Think about what makes you happy. Free time should not be the *must-be-done* time, but a *what-I-want-to-do* time. If you have something you want to do, do it. Don't fall prey to the expectations of others when it comes to your personal time. Exercise your own free will.

- What cultures do you want to know more about?

- What countries do you want to travel to?

- What other things do you want to discover?

- Or do you feel like you'd rather not do anything for a while?

Some people are afraid to allow themselves free time. They stress about how much they could do in that time. But self-care is necessary. Reward your hard work.

Have some quality free time in your life, if you don't already. Free time, again, is anything you do for your own pleasure. Whatever you do as a compulsory activity is not real free time. That is just something compulsory you do in the time when you could be doing something pleasant.

If you have never allowed yourself some self-pamper time, start small. Have just one hour of self-care time per week. Do meditation, go swimming, visit your cosmetician, or go to the movies. Then work up to five hours, then give yourself one day of free time each week. When you can afford to, take a week or two and shut out everything work-related.

Free-time activities can help you grow in so many ways. If you travel to foreign lands, learn about different cultures and understand better how others live. Broaden your horizons so you can grow as a person.

Life doesn't give you what you want, but what you deserve. So how do you make yourself deserve more? Think about it. The biggest problem is when people, even if they hate their jobs, may still like working more than what they do in their free time. Although they dream about going home and relaxing, they don't feel happy when they get there. Time spent at work still feels more valuable than the activities they do after work. If this is the case with you, make sure to change it quickly. You have only one life to live. If you feel that your free time is worthless, make it worthy. Sometimes the smallest changes can have great impacts. Try to read an adventure book instead of numbing your senses in front of HBO Family. Maybe the book will captivate you more than any movie ever could.

You feel you could use some adventure, book a cheap ticket in advance somewhere you've never been before — be it just another state, or another continent. These days, you can patch together cheap itineraries. You may need to do a little research on Google, but it will be worth it. Sometimes the excitement of the preparation is more impactful than the travel itself.

Professor Mihaly Csikszentmihalyi in his book *Flow: The Psychology of Optimal Experience* states that people are the happiest when they are in a state of concentration, deeply absorbed in what they are doing. In this state of flow, people bury themselves so deeply into the activity that nothing else seems to matter.

He divided a person's mental state into eight challenge and skill levels. If somebody has a low level of skill and challenge, then that person can slip into the state of apathy. However, if the challenge level rises (and skill level does not), then apathy can turn to worry or anxiety. For example, if a person is overweight and a bad runner, he or she doesn't have to care when they are in front of the TV. But if a huge tiger is chasing him or her, then this lack of skill could make them quite anxious. Also dead. Luckily, the probability of this event is very unlikely.

Medium-level skills with low to high challenge levels can result in boredom or arousal.

If you have strong skills in something and the stakes are not high, you may relax. With a medium challenge level, you are in control, and with high skills, you get the flow. For example, if you like drawing and you are an accomplished artist, sitting and making sketches will put you into a chilled state of mind, so you'll easily slip into a state of flow. But if you want to draw something for your spouse's birthday, you'll focus more because you'll want to make something nice. If you draw something for an exhibition or competition, the flow of artistic majesty will take you away and give you a great result. But you'll never feel apathetic or bored when you draw. You'll never hate drawing.

Based on this idea, I've collected a few pieces of advice which will help you increase the quality of your free time.

Find a hobby and build it to a high skill level.

It sounds simple — find something you like and practice it long enough to reach a high skill level. I'm sorry to say this, but great things never come easily or quickly. Passing through the low skill challenge phase is the hardest. You'll have to be persistent. You won't be the greatest tennis player in your first match, but if you're persistent, you can be the greatest in the neighborhood with time, the best in town in even longer time, and so on. This is how some people win Olympic medals — by taking a skill to the flow level.

Stay fit.

But don't do it for the sake of the tiger. If you don't like running or going to gym, do something else. Walking, biking, and swimming are all excellent forms of cardio. If you want to do something calmer, do yoga, Pilates, or any form of stretching. If you prefer team sports, collect some friends or join an existing basketball, soccer, or tennis team in your area. The point is to not let your body become lazy. It will make your brain lazy too.

Stay mentally fit.

The same applies to mental fitness. If you let your brain become lazy, your body will follow sooner or later. You have to keep both mentally and physically active. Since I am talking about free time, I don't want to give you only exercise-related advice here. Have a good book with you on your Kindle. When you have some extra time, just take it out and read. This book can be fiction, nonfiction, romance, or scientific; what matters is that you spend your free time doing something that makes you happy, and preferably a better person too.

Socialize on a flow level.

Professor Csikszentmihalyi found that the state of flow doesn't only come from work or mental activities, but also from socializing. A good conversation with friends can be very complex. An intriguing chat requires reading body language quickly, fast thinking, good vocabulary, knowledge of the topic, and also tact and diplomacy.

Free time should be filled with something that you do by choice and not by force. Think about the activities that leave you with a sense of fulfillment. Don't stress over your free time activity choices because then they become forced. If you want to play computer games for two hours, do it. Just don't expect it to give you deep satisfaction. The next day if you think back on it, you won't feel anything extraordinary like, *Wow I feel so charged from playing Solitaire yesterday*. At least a few times per week, do something that puts you in good spirits and lasts through the day after. Take a walk up a hill or spend a great evening with your loved ones.

Speaking of fulfilling activities, you can do something for your community in your free time.

In today's fast-paced, materialistic world, community goals are often considered to be a lower priority. However, a full and happy life doesn't consist only of getting, but also of giving. "Give, and it will be given to you," as the Bible says. Now, regardless of whether you are religious or not, think back to the last time you selflessly did something for somebody and that person could only give you a smile and a thank-you. Wasn't that heartwarming? It made you feel a deep sense of contentment, didn't it?

Many of the wealthiest people in the world help the needy one way or another. They donate money and established foundations for different causes. Bill Gates, the founder of Microsoft, has donated millions of dollars to good causes. He's donated $28 billion to the Bill and Melinda Gates

Foundation. Warren Buffet has promised to give 99% of his fortune to charity over time.

I could go on with examples starting with George Soros, who has his Open Society Foundations that, among other things, support kids from Africa in their quest to get a proper education. Mark Zuckerberg has donated millions of dollars to charitable causes. He also recently met Pope Francis and gifted him a drone that can expand Internet access in less connected areas. These guys helped, are helping, and will continue to help millions of people around the world.

It is admirable and respectable, but you don't need millions to contribute to society. At the heart of generosity is the desire to make a difference.

Sometimes it doesn't even cost a thing. Some kind words, a smile, or just five minutes of uninterrupted attention can work like miracles in the hearts of others. Sometimes people mistakenly think they can't make a change, that they aren't good or wealthy enough, so they don't even try. Wrong. Any little thing done for somebody else, the community, or the environment is much better than doing nothing. To you it may not seem like a great deed, but maybe to that person, it was the only kind act he experienced this month.

Don't forget, honesty plays a great role in identifying the activities that will make you truly satisfied. People often convince themselves they want things just because those things are highly appreciated in our society. Or, on the contrary, they reject things because society thinks less of it.

There are some behavior patterns that are universally recognized, like my example above — helping people in need. We can agree that this is something to be admired in a person — the willingness to help. You engage in helping others because you know it is the right thing to do. But there's a twist.

Let's say you have a well-paying job and you want to help protect the endangered lynx from extinction. In your case, the best thing you can do is not do the fieldwork yourself, placing ten feeders with food. Rather, hire fifty people to do the work more efficiently so they'll be able to place five hundred feeders with food. Unless your aim is to *look* charitable instead of *being* charitable. If this is the case, that's fine too. Just admit it (to yourself) so you can find the right motivation and fulfillment.

Whatever your real goal is, admit and accept it fully. You are not wrong when you honestly accept who you are and what your motivations are. Publius Terenicius Afer said, "I am human, I consider nothing human alien to me." If it was true in 170 BC, why wouldn't it be true today?

Maybe your goal is to be famous, or maybe is to influence a life, or a group of people, or to be well-informed about world affairs. Whatever it is, admit it, and when you are completely sure of it, pursue it!

It is essential to wake up with a real purpose every morning, a purpose that indeed makes you happy, a purpose that is yours and not someone else's expectation. And even if your purpose is directly connected to your happiness and not someone else's, but in the end makes others happy, there's nothing wrong with it.

"Be the change you want to see in the world," Gandhi said. If you start changing yourself little by little, you'll change the world too.

Let me share a personal story. I was working peacefully in a café just like I do most days. I was very focused and had tuned out my environment, but all of a sudden a hand appeared and put a little turtle figure and a card in front of me. It belonged to a deaf-mute man asking for help. He was selling the turtle for $1.50.

I recalled that I got $1.50 change back from the coffee, so I automatically put it on the table for him. I can't describe the gratefulness in his eyes. He couldn't say thank you, but his eyes and lips radiated it. I smiled back, shook his hand, and then he left. I continued my work, but I could hear two guys sitting close to me talking about how touching the scene was and how good it was to see both of us so happy with the outcome. They concluded that they wanted to do something good that day too.

As for me, it was a proof that you can always help. It doesn't matter how much or how little.

And you can be so happy! I cherish this little turtle more than any expensive gadget I've ever bought.

Free-time goals can be various, but they only give you real satisfaction if you choose them being honest with yourself, without any external influence. Free time is your time. Use it wisely.

Closing Thoughts

Your goals are overrated. And your willpower more limited than you think. But here is the good news: Except for the big things you should persist and fight for, not many temporary goals hold real meaning or value in life. Their purpose is to keep you moving. Achieving them is beside the point. You will reach many goals in your life, but you won't reach some. And that's perfectly okay. You are not a quitter, a loser, or a failure because of it.

Accepting our own limits is a tough pill to swallow, but once ingested, you'll feel much happier with yourself. After all, that never-ending pressure to always reach for something exceptional, to reach that transcendental self-actualization level, will stop burdening your mind. The stress of not always accomplishing what you've proposed will diminish.

And at the same time, accepting your own mundane limits will actually help you to focus to accomplish the things that truly matter in life. You'll realize that only a few basic habits can create a whole life-changing experience. Sometimes you don't need anything more than to learn to appreciate simple things in life, like the gifts of an old and deep friendship, helping someone in need, reading an engaging book, laughing with your love, creating something new, or running an extra mile.

I'd like to say goodbye with Zig Ziglar's words:

"What you get by achieving your goals is not as important as what you become by achieving your goals."

Yours,

Zoe

More Books By Zoe

Build Social Confidence
Find What You Were Born For
Find Who You Were Born To Be
Catching Courage
Daily Routine Makeover
Less Mess Less Stress
Minimalist Makeover
Think Different
Living Beyond Fear
Sleep Smarter
Morning Routine Makeover
Minimalist Budget
Budget Like A Pro

60073279R00083

Made in the USA
San Bernardino, CA
09 December 2017